Inventors and Creators

J.K. Rowling

Other titles in the Inventors and Creators series include:

- Alexander Graham Bell
- Walt Disney
- Thomas Edison
- Albert Einstein
- Henry Ford
- Benjamin Franklin
- Jim Henson
- Jonas Salk
- Dr. Seuss
- Steven Spielberg
- The Wright Brothers

Inventors and Creators

J.K. Rowling

P.M. Boekhoff and
Stuart A. Kallen

KIDHAVEN PRESS™

THOMSON
GALE™

San Diego • Detroit • New York • San Francisco • Cleveland
New Haven, Conn. • Waterville, Maine • London • Munich

THOMSON
GALE

Picture Credits

Cover photo: © AFP/CORBIS
Associated Press, AP, 14, 27, 33, 34, 37
© Frank Blackburn; Ecoscene/CORBIS, 10
© McPherson Colin/CORBIS SYGMA, 13, 30
© Corel Corporation, 25
© Barclay Graham/CORBIS SYGMA, 7
© Hulton/Archive by Getty Images, 8
© Murdo MacLeod/CORBIS SYGMA, 16, 23, 28
Photofest, 19, 21, 38
© Reuters NewMedia Inc./CORBIS, 40
© Geoffrey Taunton; Cordaiy Photo Library Ltd./CORBIS, 18

For more information, contact
KidHaven Press
27500 Drake Rd.
Farmington Hills, MI 48331-3535
Or you can visit our Internet site at http://www.gale.com

LIBRARY OF CONGRESS CATALOGING-IN-PUBLICATION DATA

Boekhoff, P.M. (Patti Marlene), 1957–
J.K. Rowling / by P.M. Boekhoff and Stuart A. Kallen.
p. cm.—(Inventors and creators)
Summary: Discusses the childhood, education, influences, struggles, and writing career of J.K. Rowling.
Includes bibliographical references (p.).
ISBN 0-7377-1368-2 (alk. paper)
1. Rowling, J.K.—Juvenile literature. 2. Authors, English—20th century—Biography—Juvenile literature. 3. Potter, Harry (Fictitious character)—Juvenile literature. 4. Children's stories—Authorship—Juvenile literature. I. Kallen, Stuart A., 1955– II. Title. III. Series.
PR6068 .O93 Z54 2003
823' .914—dc21

2002003292

Printed in China

Contents

Chapter One

Young Author

Joanne Rowling, better known as J.K. Rowling, is the author of the Harry Potter series, the most popular children's books ever written. Rowling's books are funny, smart, and full of surprises. They are loved by children around the world. In her stories, children escape from reality and into an imaginary world where they have great magical powers.

J.K. Rowling, known to friends and family as Jo, was born on July 31, 1965, in Chipping Sodbury, England. Jo's mother, Ann, was a lab technician and book lover, and Jo's father, Peter, was an aircraft factory manager. One of her childhood memories is of her father reading to her while she had the measles. The book he read was one of her favorites, *The Wind in the Willows*, by Scottish author Kenneth Grahame. Many of the characters in the story are talking animals, and Jo was soon inspired to write stories about talking animals, too.

Jo began making up stories at an early age. She told the tales to her younger sister Dianne, known as Di,

J.K. Rowling's inspiration has come from childhood experiences and reading books.

whom Jo describes as having a wonderful sense of humor. The sisters' favorite stories were about rabbits. "Rabbits loomed large in our early story-telling sessions; we badly wanted a rabbit. Di can still remember me telling her a story in which she fell down a rabbit hole and was fed strawberries by the rabbit family inside it."[1]

Rabbit Stories

When Jo was six years old she wrote her first story. It was called *Rabbit*, and it was a tale about a rabbit who had

Kenneth Grahame wrote *The Wind in the Willows*, one of Rowling's favorite books.

the measles. The rabbit was visited by many interesting characters, including a large bee named Miss Bee. Jo later wrote several more Rabbit stories and drew pictures to go along with them.

Even at this young age, Jo knew she wanted to be a writer when she grew up. She did not talk much about her desire to write for a living, though. She was afraid people would say that she did not have a chance of reaching her difficult goal. Jo thought her parents would just tell her to be more practical. Only Di was allowed to read the funny stories Jo wrote.

The Potters

Jo's family moved twice while she was growing up. The first move, to nearby Winterbourne, led to a friendship with Ian and Vikki Potter, a brother and sister who lived four doors down from the Rowling home. Ian loved to play tricks on the girls, such as hiding slugs on their picnic plates or convincing them to run through wet concrete.

The Potters and the Rowling sisters often dressed up and played make-believe together. During this time, Jo's favorite story was *The Little White Horse* by Elizabeth Goudge, a book her mother gave her about a little orphaned girl who finds herself in a world of magic and mystery. Inspired by the book, Jo convinced her playmates to pretend they were witches and wizards.

Jo did not have as much fun at school as she did reading and playing with the Potters. At school, her classmates made fun of her name, which sounds like "rolling."

She tired of hearing silly jokes about rolling pins. During this time, Jo decided she liked the name Potter much better than her own.

Forest of Dean

In 1974, when Jo was nine years old, her family moved again, this time to the small country village of Tutshill near the Forest of Dean, on the English-Welsh border. The Forest of Dean was a magical place, far from the city, with natural landscapes and dense, dark forests. Jo and Di enjoyed the country life, especially wandering through the fields along the Wye River.

The Wye River cuts through a valley in the Forest of Dean, an area where Rowling grew up.

Aside from exploring the countryside, Jo went to Tutshill Primary School, an old-fashioned country school with a strict teacher. Her memories of that school are not very happy, however. The teacher seated the students according to how smart she thought they were. When Jo first arrived, she was seated among the students the teachers considered least intelligent. When Jo soon proved that she was intelligent, the teacher made her change places with her new best friend. Later Jo recalled: "In one short walk across the room I became clever but unpopular."[2]

Jo looked forward to coming home from school, where she could escape into the world of books, which filled her house. Her parents allowed her to read anything she wanted. Jo loved the magical world of C.S. Lewis's Narnia series, with its themes of courage, loyalty, justice, honesty, and fairness.

Reading and Writing

As Rowling grew older she continued to read and write. However, when she was eleven years old she began to feel insecure about her appearance. Young Jo had very short hair and lots of freckles. She described herself as "short, squat, [with] very thick National Health glasses—free [government-issued] glasses that were like bottle bottoms. . . . I was shy. I was a mixture of insecurities and very bossy. Very bossy to my sister but quite quiet with strangers. Very bookish."[3]

Jo felt her classmates probably saw her as an irritating know-it-all because she raised her hand to answer every question the teacher asked. And she felt very insecure because she thought her looks were plain, so she made up for it by working hard to be the best at school.

Jo was working hard on her writing as well. When she was about twelve years old she tried writing her first novel. It was a long story about seven cursed diamonds. But the characters were not believable and it did not have much of a **plot**. Jo eventually learned the trick to writing and would later advise young authors:

> The most important thing is to read as much as you can, like I did. It will give you an understanding of what makes good writing and it will enlarge your vocabulary. And it's a lot of fun! And also, start by writing about things you know—your own experiences, your own feelings.[4]

Lunchtime Heroes

Jo still kept most of her writing secret when she went to high school at Wyedean Comprehensive. But she blended her fantasies with reality when she told funny stories to her classmates at lunchtime. Her friends were shy, serious students like herself, but in her stories they all became daring heroes. Jo was always terrible at sports, but in her stories she and her friends could do amazing physical feats that they could never perform in real life. These imaginary adventures formed a series of stories that Jo expanded upon each day.

In high school Jo traded in her thick glasses for contact lenses, and she began to feel less shy. She became happier and more comfortable with herself. She met

Rowling rushes to her next book signing at the Edinburgh International Book Festival in Scotland.

Few people knew of Rowling's early dreams of becoming a successful writer.

Sean Harris, a boy who became her best friend. Sean had a turquoise car and sometimes Jo and Sean sat in the car and talked for hours and hours. He was the only person besides her sister Di who knew about Jo's writing. And more than anything in the world, Jo wanted to be a successful author.

Chapter Two

Inspiration on a Slow Train

By the time she reached her last year of high school, Rowling was at the very top of her class. She graduated with honors in English, French, and German. Her parents encouraged her to continue studying languages so she could work as a secretary at an international company. Rowling followed her parents' advice and enrolled at Exeter University in Devon to learn how to speak fluent French.

While at Exeter Rowling earned a degree in French and studied and taught in Paris for one year. She also studied the **classic** stories of the ancient Greeks. These old books were filled with magic and heroes, along with interesting old words and good character names. During this time she continued to write many stories, but she never seemed able to finish any of them. However, she would soon come up with a story idea that would change her life.

"The Worst Secretary Ever"

After Rowling graduated from college in 1986, she moved to London to work as a secretary. She spent her

Rowling found unfulfilling jobs after she graduated from high school.

lunch hours in cafés and pubs writing short stories or putting together ideas for novels. But Rowling quickly tired of secretarial work. In fact, she called herself "the worst secretary ever, very disorganized."[5]

Rowling worked at a series of unsatisfying jobs. For a short time she even worked at a publishing company where her job was to send out rejection letters to authors whose books had been refused by the **publisher**.

In 1988 Rowling moved to Manchester to study for a teaching degree. To support herself, she worked as a secretary at the college. This job was so boring that Rowling started writing down stories and thinking up interesting character names when she was supposed to be taking notes at meetings. Later she would type up her stories in the office when her boss was not watching.

Train of Thought

Rowling used her lunch hours and spare moments to put ideas together, always working hard but never able to create a finished novel. Finally her best idea came to her in a flash of inspiration, when she was not expecting it or trying to make it happen.

In the summer of 1990 Rowling took a train from Manchester to London. The train was delayed, and a short trip turned into a four-hour journey. As she stared out the window at some cows, she suddenly had a vision of a young boy she would later call Harry Potter. She had no pen or paper with her, so she just let her imagination run wild.

She could see Harry Potter clearly in her mind, a scrawny boy with black hair and glasses, and a scar on his

Rowling thought up Harry Potter while traveling from Manchester to London on the train.

forehead. She saw him as an orphan, living with mean relatives and attending a wizard school in a castle. She thought about what the school would be like, and about the different people who would live in the castle where the school was located.

While imagining her story, Rowling decided it would take seven years to train a wizard. She saw the story of Harry Potter as one huge novel divided into seven books, one for each year of school. Rowling was very excited by the idea when it came to her, because she thought it would be so much fun to write. She later commented on the inspiration:

> I had this physical reaction to it, this huge rush of adrenaline, which is always a sign that you've had a good idea, when you've a physical response, this

> massive rush, and I'd never felt that before. I'd had ideas I liked, but never quite so powerful.[6]

By the time the train pulled into King's Cross Station four hours later, the beginning of the story and many of the characters were clear in Rowling's mind.

Writing from Experience

Rowling imagined her Harry Potter characters talking to each other. As a child, she often had imaginary conversations with witches and wizards while playing with her sister and the Potters. From the very beginning of the

Harry (left) and his uncle shield themselves from a sea of swirling invitations in a scene from *Harry Potter and the Sorcerer's Stone.*

Harry Potter books she blended the imaginary world of her childhood with the real world of her childhood, just as she had done for her lunchtime stories in school. And the characters were based on real people, though she often changed them when they became her characters. As she later said: "The book is really about the power of the imagination."[7]

Characters of Harry Potter

Hermione is the character who most resembles the author herself. Like Rowling, Hermione is smart, shy, and insecure. She loves to read and write and also cares passionately about **civil rights**.

In imagining Harry Potter, Rowling also used herself as a model. He wears glasses because Rowling wore glasses when she was young. Harry's ability to fly so well is a fulfillment of the author's fantasies about flying as a child. Through Harry, Rowling imagined what it would be like if magic were real, and what it would be like to be a real hero.

Harry's best friend Ron is based on Rowling's best friend Sean from her high school days. The magical car Harry and Ron use to fly to school is exactly the same as Sean's turquoise car. The stories that Rowling and Sean shared in that car helped the young author to accept being an outcast at school. In that car, she formed a loyal friendship that helped her transform her life, just as Ron and Harry did.

In Rowling's books school is a scary place, just as it had been for her as a child. Harry and his friends are vul-

A sorcery student attempts to fly his broomstick in a scene from *Harry Potter and the Sorcerer's Stone.*

nerable, and they are often afraid. But they have a strong sense of right and wrong, and they try to do the right thing. Using magical powers, Harry and his friends help each other beat the forces of evil.

Together they learn about tolerance, acceptance, and loyalty. They magically transform each other's lives and teach each other by sharing their special powers. And, like Rowling, they use their imaginations to look into the mysteries of the real world and try to make it a better place.

Chapter Three

Overcoming Obstacles

In 1990 J.K. Rowling imagined many of the characters and the basic plot for the entire Harry Potter series while sitting on a train. She would quickly find out, however, that dreaming up the story was the easy part. Writing it down in a solid, readable form was more difficult—and time consuming.

During the next five years, Rowling worked off and on at a series of jobs. But she spent her lunch hours sitting in pubs and cafés jotting down the Harry Potter stories. She also made drawings of the characters and scenes.

Rowling began making plans for all seven books at once, because they are all tied together by one long story. While working on one book, she scribbled down ideas that came to her for future books. During this period, Rowling created an entire world for her characters, with more details than she would ever use in her books. Although writing was now coming easier to Rowling, she would continue to experience many obstacles in her life as she created the world of Harry Potter.

Death of Her Mother

Six months after Rowling began to write the Harry Potter story, her mother died of multiple sclerosis at the age of forty-five. The twenty-five-year-old author felt her mother had always been her best friend and felt deep regret that her mother, a great book lover, never read anything Rowling wrote.

Rowling's feelings about losing her mother were soon reflected in Harry Potter's feelings about his parents' deaths. The author did not do this on purpose, and she

Rowling was saddened by the loss of her mother but continued to write her Harry Potter story.

was not aware of it while it was happening. But when she was writing, her feelings just came out. "Harry is entirely imaginary. . . . He just came out of a part of me."[8]

Teaching and Learning

Rowling continued to write her epic story through many changes in her life. In 1991, when she was twenty-six, she moved to Oporto, Portugal, to teach English. Rowling liked the job because it required her to teach only in the afternoons and evenings. In the mornings, when her mind was fresh, she had time to work on the first three chapters of the Harry Potter book. And Rowling needed this extra time because she rewrote the first chapter over and over.

> You have to resign yourself to wasting lots of trees before you write anything really good. That's just how it is. It's like learning an instrument. You've got to be prepared for hitting wrong notes occasionally, or quite a lot. That's just part of the learning process.[9]

Because Rowling wanted her book to be as perfectly written as possible, she wrote about fifteen different versions of just that first chapter.

Jessica

In 1992, while she was perfecting her book, Rowling met and married a Portuguese journalist. In 1993 her daughter Jessica was born. About three and a half

In Edinburgh (pictured), Rowling was a full-time teacher and worked hard on her first novel.

months later, Rowling's marriage ended in divorce. It was a gloomy, depressing time. Rowling was lonely and had no money, no job, and no home.

The author moved to Edinburgh, Scotland, to be near her sister Di. She arrived with her baby daughter and a suitcase half filled with Harry Potter notes and chapters. She showed her writing to her sister, and Di laughed as she had when they were children. Jo later commented: "I think I am funnier on paper than I am in person; the exact reverse of my sister who is very funny in person, but writes dull letters!"[10]

A Terrible Sadness

In Scotland Jo moved into a tiny apartment, determined to finish her book. She decided to get a degree to teach in Scotland, but since she had no money for school or child care, she went on welfare. Rowling felt hopeless and vulnerable, and she worried about providing for her child. She even cried because Jessica had so few toys; what she did have could fit inside a shoebox.

Rowling refused to feel ashamed about her financial situation, and instead wrote about her feelings of despair. During that time, her characters felt those same feelings of desperation when they were near the dementors, those who suck all the joy out of life. It was a terrible sadness. She could not imagine ever being cheerful again.

Because it is difficult for first-time authors to get their work published, Rowling doubted that she would be able to achieve her goal. But she tried not to worry about it because, for the first time in her life, she felt she had a story worth publishing. Rowling's friends helped her with money. Her sister Di encouraged her to believe that her work was good enough to be published. Rowling concentrated hard on her writing, using every bit of time to its fullest.

Every day Rowling challenged herself. She promised herself she would finish the book in one year, then try to get it published. She knew she would have to teach again soon, and she would not have the time to write with such

Despite her depression, Rowling was determined to get her first novel published.

intensity. Sometimes when Jessica fell asleep in the evening, she wrote until Jessica woke up for her morning feeding. She used her writing to turn her feelings of hopelessness into hope:

> It was pretty cold and miserable in the [apartment], so as soon as Jessica fell asleep in her

Rowling often wrote rough drafts of Harry Potter in cafés for hours at a time.

buggy, we'd head for the cafe and I'd start writing. That was probably the lowest point in my life. My self-respect was on the floor. I didn't want Jessica to grow up this way. She became my inspiration, and writing about Harry became a safe haven, someplace I could go. So, my daughter and Harry kept me going."[11]

Literary Helpers

Rowling finally completed her book, *Harry Potter and the Philosopher's Stone*, in 1995. It was the first book she had ever finished, and she felt happy having proved to herself that she could do it. She found a **literary agent** who would try to find a publisher, but he warned her that the process might take years and end unsuccessfully. While she waited, Rowling started writing her second book, which she called *Harry Potter and the Chamber of Secrets.*

As it turned out, Rowling did not have to wait very long. *Harry Potter and the Philosopher's Stone* caught the attention of editors at Bloomsbury Children's Books and they bought the **manuscript** for about $4,000 in 1996. Rowling was finally going to be a published author. She later said it was the happiest moment of her life, second only to the birth of her daughter. Bloomsbury suggested Rowling use initials for part of her name. So Rowling added a middle name, Kathleen, the name of her grandmother. From then on, she would be known as J.K. Rowling.

Though her book was published, she still did not have enough money to live. To help support herself and her daughter, the author applied for a **grant** from the Scottish

The success of Rowling's first novel allowed her to become a full-time writer.

Arts Council, which helps artists promote their work. In early 1997 the council gave her about $13,000, the largest amount they had ever given to an author of children's books. Rowling used the money to buy a computer and to pay for day care for Jessica. She also taught French part time while continuing to write the second book.

Fame and Fortune

Harry Potter and the Philosopher's Stone was finally available in British bookstores in June 1997. Children loved it so much that it became an instant success. Word spread among young readers, and soon J.K. Rowling was recognized as a major new talent in the literary world. Three months after the book was published in Britain, an American publisher bought the rights to publish the book in the United States for $105,000. It was the most money ever paid for a book by a first-time children's author.

The **advance** for the American edition made it possible for Rowling to quit her teaching job. Her lifelong desire was fulfilled; she had become a full-time writer and had enough money to take care of her daughter.

From a flash of inspiration on a train, Rowling had worked and suffered for more than five years, often fighting off sleep, cold, and despair. Now the words she had created were inspiring a new generation of young readers. Meanwhile, Harry Potter was on his way to becoming one of the most popular boys in the world.

Chapter Four

Fame and Beyond

By the end of 1997 the success of *Harry Potter and the Philosopher's Stone* made J.K. Rowling as popular as any rock star in Great Britain. This was a rare occurrence for a children's author, and Rowling was shocked by her new fame. Aggressive photographers from the British press began following her around, even camping on her doorstep. Dozens of unflattering photographs appeared in tabloid newspapers. Meanwhile, journalists wrote half-truths that exaggerated her struggle with poverty as a single mother. Such incidents made her angry and insecure and, for the first time, Rowling had trouble concentrating on her work.

Meanwhile, in July 1998, Rowling's second book, *Harry Potter and the Chamber of Secrets,* was released in Great Britain. Then in September 1998, Rowling's first book, *Harry Potter and the Philosopher's Stone,* was released in America. The American publishers, however, decided that the title might be misunderstood by readers in the United States. (Most modern Americans do not associate philosophers with magicians.) Recognizing the dilemma, Rowling suggested changing the word *philosopher* to *sorcerer,* and in America the book was renamed *Harry Potter and the Sorcerer's Stone.*

The author was delighted when this book flew to the very top of all the best-seller lists for children and adult books in the United States:

> It's incredible; it's wonderful. Initially I think one of the first reviews the first book got in America said that it wouldn't work over there. There was too much British dialect, and British slang . . . and

Adults also enjoy Rowling's books. Here a woman takes time to read *Harry Potter and the Chamber of Secrets.*

they didn't think that Harry would work over there—so ha-hah![12]

Three Best-Sellers

Rowling's third book, *Harry Potter and the Prisoner of Azkaban,* was released in Great Britain in July 1999 and in September 1999 in the United States. After this release, Rowling's three Harry Potter books occupied the first, second, and third positions on the *New York Times* best-seller list—and they stayed there for months.

As a result of her incredible success, the *New York Times* decided to create a separate best-seller list for chil-

Rowling autographs one of her books for a boy who won a Harry Potter essay contest.

dren's books. This was a great relief to some other children's authors, who would have a better chance of making the list.

In Britain Rowling won the Smarties Book Prize, the highest award for children's literature. After winning it three years in a row, Rowling finally asked that future Harry Potter titles not be considered for the award, to give others a chance to win this desirable prize.

Goblet of Fire

Rowling's fame continued to grow. But the author was experiencing great difficulties writing her fourth book, *Harry Potter and the Goblet of Fire.* This caused the author great concern because 1 million copies of the book had already been ordered by bookstores before it was even finished.

While trying to complete the book, the author discovered that the plot was not complete at a critical point in the story. To fix this glaring error, Rowling was forced to work ten-hour days for three months trying to complete the giant 734-page book. During the course of this work, she wrote thirteen versions of chapter 9 alone.

On July 8, 2000, 5.3 million copies of the new book were released—the largest first printing ever in the history of book publishing. And *Harry Potter and the Goblet of Fire* sold out in three weeks—another record. For a while, Rowling's books were in the top four spots on the *New York Times* best-seller list. And by that time, the Harry Potter books were printed in at least forty-eight languages and had sold more than 135 million copies worldwide. With sales came dozens of awards from around the world.

Helping Children

Rowling's success provided her with the opportunity to help others. Because she had struggled in the past, the author devoted time and money to the National Council for One Parent Families, an organization that helps single-parent families in Britain.

She also wrote two short books for the Comic Relief organization to help needy children in poor countries. Both books appear in the Harry Potter novels: *Fantastic Beasts and Where to Find Them* is one of Harry's textbooks, and *Quidditch Through the Ages* is a book about the sport Harry plays on a flying broomstick.

The Movies

As her popularity continued to soar, Rowling had dozens of offers from Hollywood producers who wanted to turn *Harry Potter and the Sorcerer's Stone* into a movie. The author chose to work with director Chris Columbus, who promised her he would make a movie that was as close to the book as possible.

During filming Columbus asked Rowling's opinion on nearly every aspect of the movie. She had **script** approval, which means that she had control of what the characters said and did in the movie. She wanted the movie to be filmed in Britain with British actors, and she even walked around London looking for the perfect person to play Harry Potter.

A six-year-old boy waits for his turn to participate in a Harry Potter costume contest at a mall in Indiana.

In a scene from *Harry Potter and the Sorcerer's Stone*, the three main characters are the pawns in a scary, life-size chess game.

Authors are usually not given that much power when their books are made into movies, but Rowling credits her audience with giving her that power. "I think they see me as standing in front of about a million children wanting to see it done my way. So that's what gives me any power I have."[13]

When *Harry Potter and the Sorcerer's Stone* opened in November 2001, it quickly became the most successful film of the year. A few days after the opening, Columbus began filming *Harry Potter and the Chamber of Secrets* based on Rowling's second book.

A House and a Wedding

By the time the movie was released, Rowling had become one of the world's most famous authors in the short space of four years. The author's success allowed her to buy a mansion, Killiechassie House, built in 1865 and located near the small Scottish town of Aberfeldy. On December 26, 2001, the thirty-six-year-old author married her boyfriend, Neil Murray, in a small ceremony in her new house.

After the wedding, Rowling continued to work on her fifth Harry Potter book, *Harry Potter and the Order of the Phoenix.* She continues to write nearly every day, sometimes for three hours, sometimes for ten or eleven hours, depending on how fast the ideas come to her.

Harry's World

While millions of fans eagerly await the next Harry Potter book, Rowling has already written the last chapter of

Rowling's current and future books will continue to delight and inspire young readers.

the last book. When that story is finally written, the author plans to write a Harry Potter encyclopedia with thousands of details guaranteed to please the most devoted fans. The profits of this book will be donated to charity. Until that day, J.K. Rowling will continue to live inside Harry's world and work her literary magic for children all over the world.

Notes

Chapter One: Young Author

1. J.K. Rowling, *The Not Especially Fascinating Life So Far of J.K. Rowling,* www.alexlibris.com.
2. Rowling, *The Not Especially Fascinating Life So Far of J.K. Rowling.*
3. Quoted in Linda Richards, "J.K. Rowling," *January Magazine,* October 2000, www.januarymagazine.com.
4. J.K. Rowling, online interview, Scholastic.com, February 3, 2000. www.scholastic.com/harrypotter/author.

Chapter Two: Inspiration on a Slow Train

5. Rowling, *The Not Especially Fascinating Life So Far of J.K. Rowling.*
6. Quoted in Malcolm Jones, "The Return of Harry Potter!" *Newsweek,* July 10, 2000, p. 56.
7. Quoted in Connie C. Rockman, ed., *Eighth Book of Junior Authors and Illustrators.* New York: H.W. Wilson, 2000, www.edupaperback.org.

Chapter Three: Overcoming Obstacles

8. J.K. Rowling, online interview, Comic Relief, March 12, 2001, www.scholastic.com/harrypotter/author.

9. Quoted in Richards, "J.K. Rowling."

10. J.K. Rowling, online interview, Scholastic.com, October 16, 2000. www.scholastic.com/harrypotter/author.

11. Quoted in Stephanie Loer, "Harry Potter Is Taking Publishing World by Storm," *Boston Globe*, January 3, 1999, www.nbp.org/harry.html.

Chapter Four: Fame and Beyond

12. Rowling, online interview, Comic Relief.

13. Quoted in Richards, "J.K. Rowling."

Glossary

advance: Money given by a publisher to an author before publishing the author's book.

civil rights: The basic rights of a person to experience freedom, equality, and justice.

classic: A work of art, music, or literature considered to be of the highest rank or excellence, especially one of lasting importance.

grant: Money given by organizations to help fund the work of artists, authors, scientists, and others.

literary agent: A person who sells authors' manuscripts to publishers for a share of the profits.

manuscript: A typewritten or handwritten version of a book, especially the author's own copy, prepared and submitted for publication.

plot: The main story of a book, play, movie, or other work.

publisher: A company that creates printed material for the public.

script: The written copy of a play, broadcast, or movie.

For Further Exploration

Books

David Colbert, *The Magical Worlds of Harry Potter.* Wrightsville Beach, NC: Lumina Press, 2001. The meanings behind fifty-three words Rowling uses in the Harry Potter books, including words such as alchemy and wizard.

Lindsey Fraser and J.K. Rowling, *Conversations with J.K. Rowling.* New York: Arthur A. Levine Books, 2001. J.K. Rowling's life story in her own words. The author discusses her birth in Chipping Sodbury, her teachers, and her first fan letter.

Philip Nel, *J.K. Rowling's Harry Potter Novels: A Reader's Guide.* New York: Continuum, 2001. Discusses the plot and characters found in the Harry Potter stories and why readers love the books.

Kenneth Grahame, *The Wind in the Willows.* New York: Baronet Books, 1994. The story of a shy mole and a water rat and their adventures in the wild woods.

Allan Zola Kronzek and Elizabeth Kronzek, *The Sorcerer's Companion: A Guide to the Magical World of Harry Potter.* New York: Broadway Books, 2001. Explores the true history and mythology behind the magical practices that appear in the Harry Potter books.

C.S. Lewis, The Chronicles of Narnia. New York: HarperCollins, 1994. Seven books about four children who travel to a world where they become powerful people and use faith and hope to fight evil.

J.K. Rowling, *Harry Potter and the Sorcerer's Stone.* New York: Arthur A. Levine Books, 1998. Harry Potter's first year at Hogwarts School for Wizards and Witches.

J.K. Rowling, *Harry Potter and the Chamber of Secrets.* New York: Arthur A. Levine Books, 1999. Harry Potter faces danger from a dark power released on Hogwarts School when the Chamber of Secrets is opened again.

J.K. Rowling, *Harry Potter and the Prisoner of Azkaban.* New York: Arthur A. Levine Books, 1999. Harry Potter confronts the dangerous wizard responsible for the deaths of his parents.

J.K. Rowling, *Harry Potter and the Goblet of Fire.* New York: Arthur A. Levine Books, 2000. Fourteen-year-old Harry Potter goes to the Quidditch World Cup with the Weasleys, and he is mysteriously entered in a contest with an old enemy that has grown stronger.

J.K. Rowling, *Fantastic Beasts and Where to Find Them.* New York: Arthur A. Levine Books, 2001. About the mythical animals and monsters in the wizard world written by the fictitious author Newt Scamander.

J.K. Rowling, *Quidditch Through the Ages.* New York: Arthur A. Levine Books, 2001. Fictitious Hogwarts library book about the history of the sport of quidditch written by the fictitious author Kennilworthy Whisp.

Website

J.K. Rowling **The Not Especially Fascinating Life So Far of J.K. Rowling**. (www.alexlibris.com). J.K. Rowling describes her life in her own words, including her education, childhood, and many jobs.

Index